JOHN RUTTER

MASS OF THE CHILDREN

FOR SOPRANO AND BARITONE SOLI,
CHILDREN'S CHOIR, MIXED CHOIR,
AND ORCHESTRA

MUSIC DEPARTMENT

OXFORD
UNIVERSITY PRESS

OXFORD

UNIVERSITY PRESS

Great Clarendon Street, Oxford OX2 6DP, England
198 Madison Avenue, New York, NY 10016, USA

Oxford University Press is a department of the University of Oxford.
It furthers the University's aim of excellence in research, scholarship,
and education by publishing worldwide in

Oxford New York
Auckland Cape Town Hong Kong Karachi
Kuala Lumpur Madrid Melbourne Mexico City Nairobi
New Delhi Shanghai Taipei Toronto

With offices in

Argentina Austria Brazil Chile Czech Republic France Greece
Guatemala Hungary Italy Japan Poland Portugal Singapore
South Korea Switzerland Thailand Turkey Ukraine Vietnam

Oxford is a registered trade mark of Oxford University Press
in the UK and in certain other countries

ISBN 978-0-19-338094-3

Printed in Great Britain on acid-free paper

Front cover based on an original design by Richard Craddock

CONTENTS

Mass of the Children was written at the invitation of Peter Tiboris and MidAmerica Productions, under whose auspices the first performance was given on 13 February 2003 in Carnegie Hall, New York, conducted by the composer.

It was first recorded by the Cambridge Singers, Cantate Youth Choir, and the City of London Sinfonia, with soloists Joanne Lunn and Roderick Williams, conducted by the composer. The recording is on the Collegium label (COLCD 129).

For texts, see p. 60. A programme note is available on the Collegium website:
www.collegium.co.uk

A separate children's choir part with keyboard reduction is also available
(ISBN 978-0-19-338095-1)

Duration: 37 minutes

INSTRUMENTATION

Mass of the Children is available in two different instrumentations (both intended for players of good standard):

1. **for orchestra:**

> 2 flutes
> 2 oboes
> 2 clarinets in B flat
> 2 bassoons
> 2 horns in F
> 2 trumpets in B flat
> 3 pedal timpani (1 player)
> percussion*
> harp
> strings

> *2 players: glockenspiel, crotales, tubular bells, bell tree, suspended cymbal, clash cymbals, snare drum, tenor drum, tambourine

2. **for chamber ensemble with organ:**

> flute
> oboe
> clarinet in B flat
> bassoon
> horn in F
> 3 pedal timpani (1 player)
> percussion*
> harp
> double bass
> organ

> *1 or 2 players: as for orchestral version

All performing material for both versions is available on hire from Oxford University Press. Please specify, when ordering, which version is required.

MASS OF THE CHILDREN

JOHN RUTTER

1. Kyrie

*Words by Thomas Ken (1637–1711)

Printed in Great Britain

OXFORD UNIVERSITY PRESS, MUSIC DEPARTMENT, GREAT CLARENDON STREET, OXFORD OX2 6DP

*In bars 59–66, the lowest voice is optional, but in bars 67–70 the voices should divide into three as shown.

2. Gloria

*Tenors could sing in unison with basses in bars 49–56 if desired.

gloria, gloria, gloria, glo - ri - a in ex - cel - sis De - o,

G

Half speed – tranquillo (♩ = 69)

et___ in ter - ra pax, in ter - ra pax ho - mi - ni - bus, ho - mi - ni - bus bo - nae vo - lun -

et___ pax, pax,

G

Half speed – tranquillo (♩ = 69)

*It is suggested that both the 1st and 2nd voices should consist of a mixture of sopranos and altos.

21

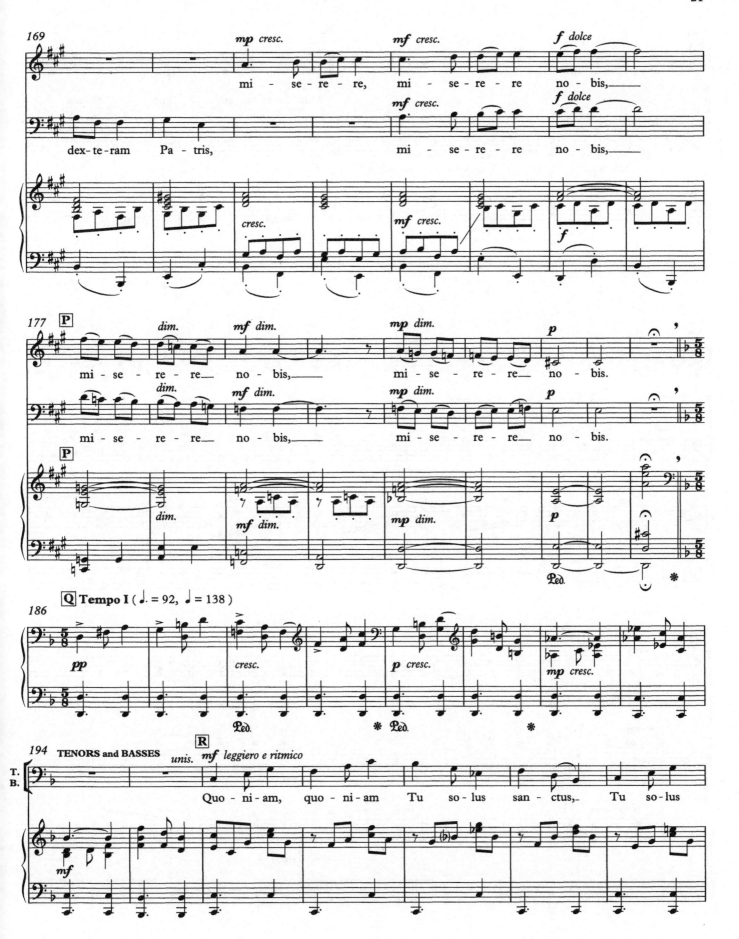

3. Sanctus and Benedictus

27

4. Agnus Dei

* Text by William Blake (1757–1827)

thou a lamb, We are call - ed by his name. Lit - tle lamb, God bless thee,

(SOPRANOS)
God

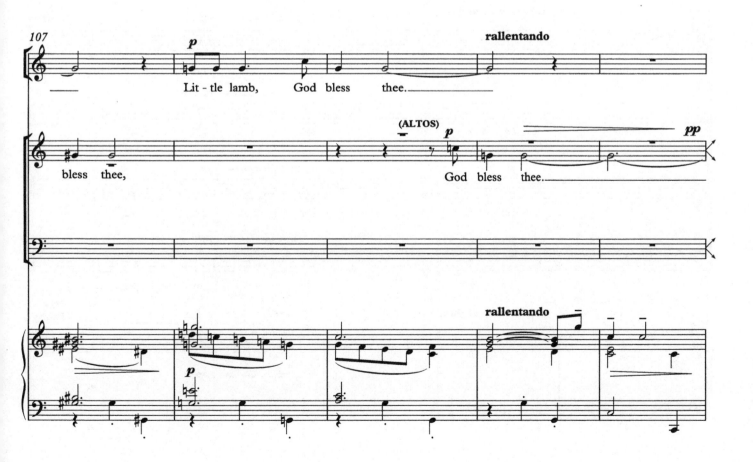

bless thee,

Lit - tle lamb, God bless thee.

(ALTOS)
God bless thee.

5. Finale (Dona nobis pacem)

*Text by the composer, based on a prayer of Lancelot Andrewes (1555–1626)

*Text by the composer, based on St Patrick's Breastplate (5th century)
†If preferred, chorus may hum from here to bar 59.

48

50

*Text by Thomas Ken (1637–1711)

†If preferred, the alto part in the children's choir from here to the end may be sung an octave higher.

59

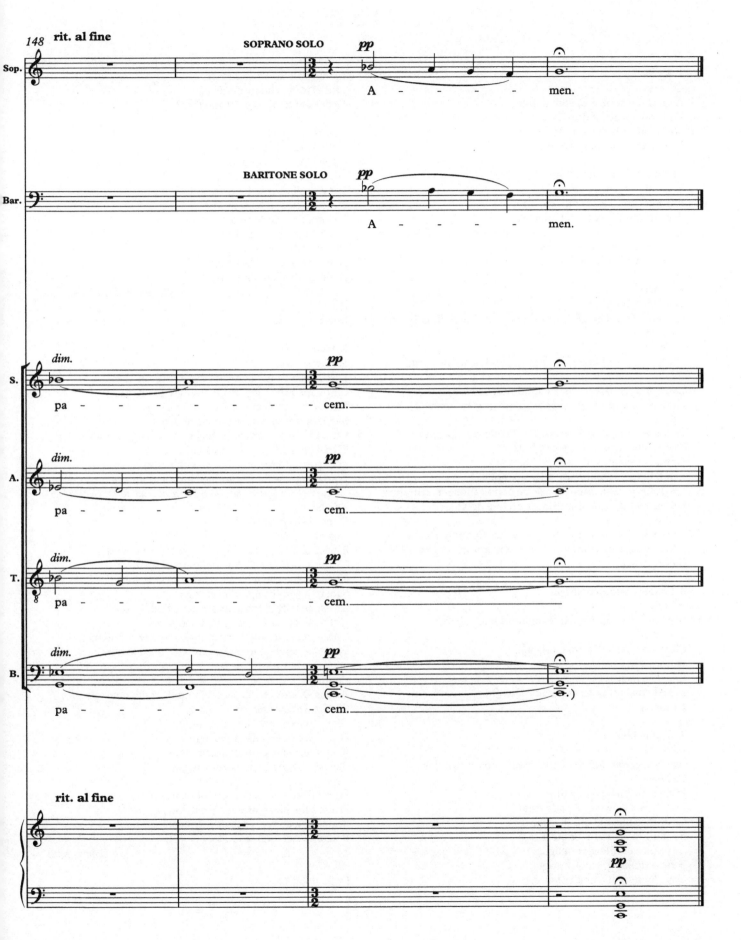

Printed by Halstan

TEXTS

1. Kyrie

Children:
Awake my soul, and with the sun
Thy daily stage of duty run;
Shake off dull sloth, and joyful rise
To pay thy morning sacrifice.

Redeem thy mis-spent time that's past,
Live this day as if 'twere thy last:
Improve thy talent with due care;
For the great Day thyself prepare.

(Thomas Ken, 1637–1711)

Adults (then children and soloists):
Kyrie eleison. Christe eleison. Kyrie eleison.

2. Gloria

Children, then adults:
Gloria in excelsis Deo, et in terra pax hominibus bonae voluntatis.
Children:
Glory be to God in highest heaven, and peace on earth.
Adults:
Laudamus te, benedicimus te, adoramus te.
Gratias agimus tibi propter magnam gloriam tuam.
Soloists:
Domine Deus, Rex caelestis, Deus Pater omnipotens.
Domine Fili unigenite, Jesu Christe.
Domine Deus, Agnus Dei, Filius Patris,
Qui tollis peccata mundi, miserere nobis.
Qui tollis peccata mundi, suscipe deprecationem nostram.
Qui sedes ad dexteram Patris, miserere nobis.
Adults:
Quoniam Tu solus sanctus, Tu solus Dominus, Tu solus Altissimus, Jesu Christe, Cum Sancto Spiritu in gloria Dei Patris. Amen.

3. Sanctus and Benedictus

Adults:
Sanctus, Sanctus, Sanctus Dominus Deus Sabaoth,
Hosanna!
Pleni sunt caeli et terra gloria tua.
Hosanna in excelsis.
Children, then adults and soloists:
Benedictus qui venit in nomine Domini.
Hosanna!

4. Agnus Dei

Adults:
Agnus Dei, qui tollis peccata mundi, miserere nobis.
Children:
Little lamb, who made thee?
Dost thou know who made thee?
Gave thee life and bid thee feed,
By the stream and o'er the mead;
Gave thee clothing of delight,
Softest clothing, woolly bright;
Gave thee such a tender voice,

Making all the vales rejoice:
Little lamb, who made thee?
Dost thou know who made thee?

Adults and children:
Little lamb, I'll tell thee;
Little lamb, I'll tell thee:
He is called by thy name,
For he calls himself a Lamb:
He is meek and he is mild,
He became a little child:
I a child and thou a lamb,
We are called by his name.
Little lamb, God bless thee.
Little lamb, God bless thee.

(William Blake, 1757–1827)

Adults:
Miserere nobis.

5. Finale

Baritone soloist:
Lord, open thou mine eyes that I may see thee;
Lord, open thou my lips that I may praise thee;
Lord, open thou my heart that I may love thee,
Serve thee with joy, fear none above thee.
Christ be my sword and shield, my strong defender;
Christ be my light and my Redeemer.
Lord, be with me this day in each endeavour;
Lord, keep my soul with thee now and for ever.

(John Rutter, based on Lancelot Andrewes, 1555–1626)

Adults:
Dona nobis pacem.
Soprano soloist:
Christ, be my guide today, my guide tomorrow;
Christ in my days of joy, my days of sorrow;
Christ in the silent hours when I lie sleeping,
Safe in his holy angels' keeping.
Christ be within the hearts of all who love me;
Christ all around, and Christ above me.
Christ in my thought and prayer and my confessing;
Christ, when I go to rest, grant me your blessing.

(John Rutter, based on St Patrick's Breastplate, 5th cent.)

Adults:
Agnus Dei, qui tollis peccata mundi, dona nobis pacem.
Children, at the same time:
Glory to thee, my God, this night
For all the blessings of the light;
Keep me, O keep me, King of kings,
Beneath thy own almighty wings.

Praise God, from whom all blessings flow,
Praise him, all creatures here below,
Praise him above, ye heavenly host,
Praise Father, Son, and Holy Ghost.

(Thomas Ken)

All:
Dona nobis pacem.